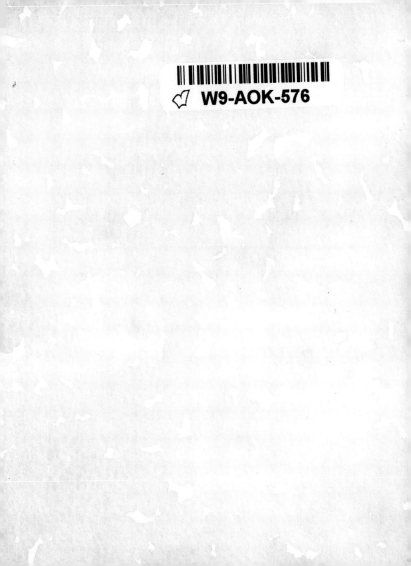

THE MINIATURE BOOK OF
Flowers as Food

MARY LAWRENCE &
JANE NEWDICK

Published by Salamander Books Limited
LONDON • NEW YORK

Published by Salamander Books Limited
129-137 York Way, London N7 9LG, United Kingdom

© Salamander Books Ltd., 1991

ISBN 0 86101 526 6

Distributed by Hodder & Stoughton Services, P.O. Box 6,
Mill Road, Dunton Green, Sevenoaks, Kent TN13 2XX

All correspondence concerning the content of this volume
should be addressed to Salamander Books Ltd.

CREDITS

MANAGING EDITOR: *Jilly Glassborow*
EDITED BY: *Veronica Ross*
PHOTOGRAPHY BY: *Di Lewis and Richard Paines*
DESIGN AND ARTWORK BY: *Pauline Bayne*
TYPESET BY: *SX Composing Ltd.*
COLOUR SEPARATION BY: *P&W Graphics, Pte. Ltd.*
PRINTED IN BELGIUM BY: *Proost International Book Production,
Turnhout, Belgium*

CONTENTS

INTRODUCTION 8

SUMMER SALAD 10

HYSSOP & BEAN SALAD 12

GERANIUM MELON 14

SALAD BURNETT SAVOURY 16

ROSE VINAIGRETTE 18

BORAGE SOUP 20

MARIGOLD CAULIFLOWER 22

CHICKEN & THYME 24

MARIGOLD FILLETS 26

ELDERFLOWER FRITTERS 28

'PINK' PEARS 30

ROSE DESSERT 32

MARIGOLD CAKE 34

GERANIUM JELLY 36

TRUFFLES 38

ELDERFLOWER CUP 40

CLARET PUNCH 42

TISANES & TEAS 44

INTRODUCTION

The recent emphasis on presenting food that is as good to look at as it is to eat has encouraged a revival in the art of cooking with flowers. Garnishing with flowers and herbs has long been popular and a random scattering of petals or leaves can transform the appearance of a dish, but many of the recipes in this book use flowers as a major ingredient as well. The final results are extremely good and the subtle flavours and textures that flowers can introduce to a dish suit the modern move towards light, simple flavours and fresh, natural food.

Any garden, whatever size it may be, will provide enough space to grow a selection of flowers for the kitchen. Hyssop, thyme, marjoram and rosemary can all be used for their leaves as well as their flowers. Nasturtiums and marigolds are superb in salads and add a splash of brilliant colour and a delicious spicy flavour. Roses can be used in summer puddings to add a subtle aroma as well as a pretty garnish. Elder blossoms are traditionally used to make a sparkling country drink, and scented geraniums make the most delicious preserves, while dried flowers can be used to make fragrant teas.

The flowers you choose for your recipes should be fresh, unblemished and unsprayed. Check carefully for insects and, if you wash the flowerheads, do so carefully as the delicate petals can bruise easily. If you decide to experiment with different types of flowers do check first that they are edible, as some flowers are poisonous. Remember, too, that some wild-flowers are scarce, so only pick common species, growing in abundance.

These creative recipes add a new dimension to food preparation and certainly give the home cook the chance to experiment. Try making some of the recipes in this book or use flowers to liven up a favourite dish – you could be pleasantly surprised.

*S*UMMER SALAD

Mixed lettuce leaves
About 36 nasturtium heads

Dressing
2 tablespoons olive oil
1 tablespoon walnut oil
1 teaspoon made French mustard
1 tablespoon white wine vinegar
Salt & ground pepper

*N*asturtiums add a peppery taste to a green or mixed salad and a flash of contrasting colour. This attractive summer salad, rich in vitamin C, can be eaten as a first course or on its own.

The nasturtium flowers should be fresh, unblemished and unsprayed. Do not wash them if possible, as the petals bruise easily. Check in the long horn at the back for insects and pick off the stem. Mix the flowers with the lettuce leaves. Shake the dressing ingredients together and mix with the salad just before serving. Serves 6.

HYSSOP & BEAN SALAD

1¼lb (600g) salad potatoes, cooked and cooled
10oz (300g) french beans, cooked and cooled
2oz (60g) black olives
8oz (250g) cherry tomatoes
2 tablespoons chopped fresh hyssop flowers & leaves
Sprigs fresh hyssop flowers, to decorate

Dressing
3 tablespoons olive oil
1 tablespoon lemon juice
1 crushed garlic clove
Salt & ground pepper

In midsummer take advantage of the abundant supplies of vegetables to make this tasty and colourful salad. Gently mix all the salad ingredients together and put in an earthenware dish. Blend together the ingredients for the dressing and pour over the salad just before serving. Decorate with the brilliant-blue hyssop blooms.

GERANIUM MELON

~

1 small water melon
10 fl oz (300ml/1¼ cups) water
2½oz (75g/⅓ cup) caster sugar
2 strips lemon peel
4 borage (borago) leaves
Juice of 1 lemon & 1 lime
Geranium & borage flowers, to decorate

This colourful and pretty combination of fruit and flowers makes a wonderfully refreshing starter for a light lunch. Slice off the top of the water melon. Carefully extract the fruit and remove the pips. Roughly chop the fruit into cubes, and mix with the water, sugar, lemon peel and borage leaves. Transfer this mixture to a saucepan and simmer for a few minutes to allow the flavours to combine but do not let the fruit become mushy. Strain the mixture and allow to cool. Add the lemon and lime juice and spoon the mixture back into the water melon. Decorate with a few scented geranium and borage flowers and for an extra special occasion serve the melon on a bed of vine leaves. Serves 1.

SALAD BURNETT SAVOURY

❧

Equal amounts of cottage cheese & cream cheese
Salad burnett (burnet) leaves & flowers
Fennel flowers
Olive oil
Salt & ground pepper
Melba toast

Salad burnett, fennel flowers and a little black pepper combined with soft cheeses, produces this delightfully refreshing savoury which can be served as a starter or at the end of a meal. Strip the leaves from salad burnett stems and wash well. Chop the leaves finely and place in a bowl with the fennel flowers, a teaspoon of olive oil and salt and pepper to taste. Leave for 30 minutes and then add the cottage cheese and cream cheese and beat with a fork. Lightly oil the insides of ramekins or small bowls, and fill with the cheese mixture. Chill well and then turn out and decorate with fennel florets and serve with Melba toast. Serves 4.

ROSE VINAIGRETTE

∽

1 cup rose wine vinegar
1 cup sunflower oil
1 teaspoon of sugar
4 pink roses
Red & pink roses for decoration

Globe artichokes make appetising starters and look especially attractive served on a bed of rose petals with rose-petal vinaigrette. Some varieties of rose-petal are sweeter than others, so taste those you intend to use.

Cook the artichokes in boiling salted water until tender. To test, lift from the pan and pull away one of the leaves – if it comes away easily it is cooked. Drain upside down in a colander. Cut off the white bitter part at the base of each rosé-petal and put in a bowl. Boil the wine vinegar in a pan and add the sugar. Pour this mixture over the rose petals and leave to stand for about 4 hours. Strain and add the sunflower oil. Pour into a glass jug and decorate with a few rose petals. Serves 4.

$\mathscr{B}$ORAGE SOUP

½lb (250g) young borage (Borago) leaves & flowers
2oz (60g/⅓ cup) short grain rice
2oz (60g/¼ cup) butter
1½ pints (900ml/3¾ cups) chicken or vegetable stock
6oz (175g/¾ cup) double cream (or fromage frais)
Seasoning to taste

*T*his dark green soup served cold is perfect for summer dinner parties or that extra special picnic. Melt the butter in a saucepan. Add the rice and cook over a low heat for two minutes, stirring all the time. Add the stock and simmer for 15 minutes. Strip the borage leaves and flowers from the stalks and wash well. Leave aside some flowers for decoration and add the remainder to the saucepan. Simmer for a further 10 minutes. Season to taste. Allow to cool for a while, then liquidize in a blender. Pour the soup through a fine sieve into a serving tureen and allow to cool. Before serving stir in the cream or if preferred some thinned fromage frais, and decorate with the bright blue borage flowers. Serves 4.

MARIGOLD CAULIFLOWER

~

1 medium sized cauliflower
2oz (60g/¼ cup) butter
2oz (60g/½ cup) plain white flour
3oz (90g/⅓ cup)) grated cheese
½pt (300ml/1¼ cups) milk
6 heads pot marigolds
Salt & pepper

Marigolds are such bright and cheerful flowers, and as well as being good to look at they can also be good to eat. They have a subtle spicy flavour which can transform this favourite dish into something special. Make the white sauce in the usual manner. Carefully wash the marigold flowers in cold running water and shake dry. Reheat the white sauce and stir in the grated cheese while over the heat, but do not allow to boil. Remove from heat, and add in the marigold petals. Stir carefully. Place the lightly cooked cauliflower into a serving dish and pour the sauce over the top. Serves 4.

CHICKEN & THYME

Skinned chicken breasts
Long stems of thyme in bloom
Bunch fresh thyme
3 tablespoons corn oil
Juice of two lemons
Salt & pepper

Chicken cooked with thyme tastes delicious and this appetising dish is the perfect choice for an informal summer lunch or barbecue party. Chop or grind the bunch of thyme, and mix with the corn oil, lemon juice and seasoning in a large bowl. Add the chicken pieces to the mixture and leave to marinate for two hours, turning the chicken occasionally. Remove the chicken just before cooking and allow to drain, but make sure plenty of chopped thyme is left on the chicken pieces. Cook the chicken over a medium hot barbecue for approximately 20 minutes. For extra flavour dip the long stems of flowering thyme into the marinade and lay over the chicken while the underside is cooking.

MARIGOLD FILLETS

Fillets of smoked mackerel or herring
Small green lettuce

Sauce
2 tablespoons sunflower oil
4 tablespoons cider vinegar
2 heaped teaspoons grated horseradish
8 heads marigold flowers

Serve succulent smoked mackerel or herring fillets on a bed of orange marigold flowers and crisp green lettuce for a winning summer party dish. Measure the cider vinegar into a mixing bowl, add the grated horseradish and crush well with a wooden spoon. Blend in the sunflower oil and leave to infuse for 30 minutes. Wash the marigold flowers and drain well. Cut the mackerel fillets in half lengthways and arrange in a star shape on a bed of lettuce. Stir the marigold petals into the sauce and spoon some of the sauce and petals between the fillets. Serve the rest of the sauce separately. Serves 4.

ℰLDERFLOWER FRITTERS

❧

Elderflower sprays (Sambucus nigra) just open
2 eggs
2oz (60g/½ cup) plain flour
½ pt (300ml/1¼ cups)) of milk
Icing sugar
Oil for deep frying

ℰ lderflowers, seen in abundance along the hedgerows in spring, can be used to make an interesting and unusual after dinner dessert. Examine the sprays carefully for insects, and shake well but do not wash. Sift the flour into a bowl. Make a well in the centre and drop in the egg yolks. Draw the flour into the yolks, while gradually adding the milk. Beat the batter until it is the consistency of single cream. Heat the oil in a deep pan. Dip the flower heads into the batter. Shake off the excess and, holding onto the stalk, deep fry the flower head for two minutes. Dry on kitchen paper. Cut off the stalks just before serving and dust with icing sugar. Serve hot or cold. Serves 4.

'PINK' PEARS

6 firm pears
½ bottle red wine
18 garden pinks (Dianthus)
½pt (300ml/1¼ cups) double cream
2 tablespoons milk
Sugar

This elegant dish is a perfect summer dessert. Wash the pinks carefully and shake dry. Remove the petals from 12 flowers and place in a saucepan with the wine and sugar to taste. Bring to the boil. Peel the pears, but leave on the stalks. Place in the saucepan and leave to simmer for 20 minutes, turning so that all sides colour evenly. Remove the pears, and reduce the liquid to make a thick sauce. Allow to cool. Heat the milk in a double saucepan and add the petals from the remaining 6 pinks. Heat to just below boiling point for 5 minutes. Remove from the heat and allow to stand for 15 minutes then strain the milk into a bowl. Add a teaspoon of sugar, allow to dissolve, then pour in cream and beat to a stiff consistency. Serve pears with the sauce poured over. Serves 6.

ROSE DESSERT

❧

10fl oz (300ml/1¼ cups) whipping cream
(or half cream, half fromage frais)
1½ tablespoons gelatine
4 tablespoons water
2 large eggs, separated
2oz (60g/¼ cup) caster sugar
10fl oz (300ml/1¼ cups) Greek yoghurt
2 tablespoons triple-distilled rose water
Petals and flowers, to decorate

This soft light pudding is slightly scented and flavoured with roses. It combines beautifully with the tender red fruits of summer – strawberries, redcurrants, cherries and raspberries. Whip the cream lightly. Dissolve the gelatine in the water. Beat the egg yolks and sugar with an electric whisk until thick and fluffy, then beat in the yoghurt. Whisk the egg whites. Beat the cool gelatine into the egg-yolk mixture and, working rapidly, add the rose water, cream and beaten egg whites. Pour into a dish and chill for several hours before decorating. Serves 6.

MARIGOLD CAKE

8oz (250g/1 cup) softened butter
8oz (250g/1 cup) caster sugar
4 eggs, beaten
8oz (250gm/2 cups) plain flour
1 teaspoon baking powder
Grated rind of 1 orange & 1 lemon
3 tablespoons fresh marigold petals
or 2 tablespoons dried
Granulated sugar (optional)

Marigold petals give a delicate flavour and a slight orange hue to this light tea-time cake. Grease and line a 2lb (1kg) loaf tin. Cream the butter with the sugar and add the beaten egg a little at a time. Sieve the flour with the baking powder and fold into the creamed mixture. Add in the orange and lemon rinds and the marigold petals. Spoon into the tin and bake in a oven preheated to 350°F (180°C or Mark 4) for about 1 hour. Sprinkle with granulated sugar about half-way through if desired. Cool for 5 minutes, then remove from the tin. Serve when just cool. This cake keeps well and can be frozen.

GERANIUM JELLY

~

4lb (2kg) cooking apples
1¾ pints (1 litre/4 cups) water
Granulated or preserving sugar
Juice of 2 lemons
15 scented geranium leaves

There are many different types of scented geraniums but rose- and lemon-scented varieties are the best for making these delicious preserves. Serve at teatime with good bread and butter or plain scones.

Chop the apples roughly, leaving the skin, stalk and pips. Put in a large pan with the water and simmer until soft. Strain for several hours through a jelly bag or muslin; do not squeeze the fruit through or the jelly will be cloudy. Measure the juice into a preserving pan and for every pint (600ml) of juice add 1lb (450g/4 cups) of sugar. Add the lemon juice and the geranium leaves. Stir over a low heat to dissolve the sugar, then boil rapidly for about 10 minutes, until set. Quickly remove the leaves and pour into clean, warm jars.

*T*RUFFLES

～

6oz (175g) white or plain chocolate, for centres
2 tablespoons single cream
1 egg yolk
1 tablespoon brandy &
1 tablespoon rose water
or 2 tablespoons violet liqueur
6oz (175g) white or plain chocolate, for coating
Crystallised petals to decorate

*T*hese delicious truffles are made from the same basic mixture, but the rose version has a dark rose-scented truffle centre covered with white chocolate, and the violet version a white, violet-scented centre encased in plain chocolate.

Gently melt the chocolate (for the centres) into the cream. Add the egg yolk, liqueur and flavouring. Remove from the heat and cool. Roll the mixture into small balls and leave to harden. Melt the coating chocolate gently over hot water and dip each truffle in until well coated. Leave on an oiled surface and decorate with crystallised petals before set. The mixture makes about 15 truffles.

*E*LDERFLOWER CUP

~~~

6 elderflower heads (Sambucus nigra)
1½lb (700g/3 cups) white sugar
3 lemons
2 tablespoons white wine vinegar
8 pints (4.5 litres) water
Elderflower sprigs, to decorate

*I*n summer the frothy, creamy elderflower blossoms can be used to produce elderflower 'champagne', a sparkling, refreshing drink that can be enjoyed on any lazy summer's day. Dissolve the sugar in a little of the water heated to boiling point. Thinly pare the lemons and add the peel to the sugar. Wash the elderflower heads well to remove all insects and place in a large glass bowl. Add the sugar and peel mixture, the wine vinegar and the remaining water. Stir well, cover and leave for about 4 days in a cool place. In around 5 days it should be sparkling and ready to drink. Serve well chilled in tall glasses. Makes 9 pints (5 litres).

CLARET PUNCH

1 tablespoon caster sugar
8oz (250g) fresh strawberries
4 small strips cucumber peel
Juice of 3 lemons
3 tablespoons brandy
2 tablespoons Cointreau
2 bottles claret or similar red wine
1 bottle sparkling mineral water, soda or lemonade
Borage (Borago) flowers & mint

This delicious cherry-red wine cup is best served from a clear glass bowl to appreciate the sparkling colour and the pretty decoration. Dissolve the caster sugar in a little hot water and pour into a large bowl. Slice the strawberries if they are large, and add to the bowl together with the cucumber strips, lemon juice, brandy and Cointreau. Pour in the 2 bottles of red wine and top up with the mineral water, soda or lemonade. Chill well. When ready to serve, add ice and decorate with a liberal sprinkling of borage flowers and mint sprigs. Serves 20.

TISANES & TEAS

∾

Good quality loose tea
Rose petals
White jasmine
Bergamot (Monarda)
Lime
Marigold
Camomile (Anthemis)

*A*s well as adding scent and flavour to conventional teas, flowers can be used to make tisanes. Use 1 teaspoon of dried flowers or 3 teaspoons of fresh per cup, and steep them for about 3 or 4 minutes before drinking. Make in a jug and strain into a cup.

Make your own exotic teas by adding dried petals to loose tea. Simply mix the tea with the petals. Try strongly scented red rose petals or dried flowers from the common white jasmine. The proportion of petals to tea will depend on how strong you want the flower flavour to be. Experiment with 2 tablespoons of rose petals to 3½oz (100g/6 tablespoons) of tea, and 1 tablespoon of the stronger scented jasmine to 3½oz (100g/6 tablespoons) tea.